really important stuff my kids have taught me

CYNTHIA L. COPELAND

W9-BRM-293

WORKMAN PUBLISHING · NEW YORK

For my mother, who has taught me almost
as much as my children have

Library of Congress Cataloging-in-Publication Data is available.

ISBN 978-0-7611-8551-2

Design by Jennifer K. Beal Davis and Lisa Hollander
Photo research by Michael Dimascio
Front cover photo by Chuck Schmidt/E+/Getty Images
Back cover photo by Jamie Grill/Tetra Images/Getty Images

Workman books are available at special discounts when purchased in bulk
for premiums and sales promotions as well as for fund-raising or educational
use. Special editions or book excerpts can also be created to specification.
For details, contact the Special Sales Director at the address below, or send
an email to specialmarkets@workman.com.

Workman Publishing Company, Inc.
225 Varick Street
New York, NY 10014-4381
workman.com

WORKMAN is a registered trademark of Workman Publishing Co., Inc.

Printed in China
First printing July 2015

10 9 8 7 6 5 4 3 2 1

contents

Don't tell my kids this, but they've taught me a lot more than I've taught them.

When they were small, I was amazed at the insight and clarity they brought to issues I was still struggling to understand. My red-cheeked daughter in her wet snowsuit couldn't define persistence or discuss its value as a character trait, but she had figured out that if she wanted in, she had to keep banging until someone opened the door. Her younger sister hadn't studied the art of presentation and persuasion, but she knew that wearing pajamas with feet would not help her win an argument for a later bedtime. And my son often reminded me that a little kiss could make a big difference. It's been more than two decades since the original edition of this book was published, and my children, now in their twenties, continue to inspire and enlighten me.

My children, their pet chickens, and our dog, Bear, circa 1997

If you're fortunate enough to have your own young children, continue to appreciate their wisdom. If not, turn off your cell phone the next time you are sitting on a park bench and tune in to the conversation in the sandbox. You just might learn a thing or two.

I've gathered within the following pages an assortment of smart, funny, innocent, perfectly sensible things my kids have taught me over the years. Read on and remind yourself how simple everything really is.

Cindy Copeland

1

cheer!

Children are just *more:* more joyful, more enthusiastic, more curious, more outspoken. They laugh longer, hug harder, and yell louder. They fully embrace what is happening in the moment, untroubled by voices from the past or concerns about the future.

Because they experience life as one exciting surprise after another, kids jump at the chance to try new things, and they celebrate even the smallest successes. A backward somersault? Hooray! Leaping off a swing at the very top of its arc? Whoopee! They look for reasons to laugh out loud and dance with abandon. To a child, simply seeing the sun come up in the morning is a reason to cheer.

Recess is the BEST PART.

Tickle your own funny bone.

Even before we can talk, we can laugh. At four or five months old, we begin to chuckle in response to those around us. Laughter is about our human connections; how much we laugh depends on how much time we spend with other people. Young children laugh more than adults because they tend to have more social interactions. The things that make kids laugh relate to their development (think peek-a-boo for a one-year-old and nonsense words for a pre-schooler) until the fourth or fifth grade, when studies show that boys and girls begin to find different things funny. One thing everyone can agree on: Sharing a belly laugh with friends is one of life's great joys.

Never, EVER miss the fireworks on the Fourth of July.

Make up
a reason
to have a
PARTY.

Don't worry about crossing the street until you get to the curb.

Sometimes you have to scream on the way down.

ONE HUNDRED TIMES
is not too many
when it's your
FAVORITE BOOK.

Play, don't watch.

Thirteen-year-old Mo'ne Davis captivated the country at the 2014 Little League World Series, where she became the first female pitcher to throw a shutout (and only the eighteenth girl to play in the Series). Pitching for the Taney Dragons of Philadelphia, Mo'ne took her team to the semifinals and became the first Little Leaguer to appear on the cover of *Sports Illustrated.* Despite the fact that the governor of Pennsylvania predicted she would someday play professional baseball, her dream is to play basketball at UConn!

According to Mo'ne Davis,
"Throwing 70 miles an hour,
that's *throwing like a girl.*"

Learn it by heart.

A snow day is more fun than a vacation day.

"As long as this exists, this sunshine and this cloudless sky, and as long as I can enjoy it, how can I be sad?"

—ANNE FRANK,
THE DIARY OF A YOUNG GIRL

go
barefoot

Take it apart to
SEE HOW IT WORKS.

Collect things.

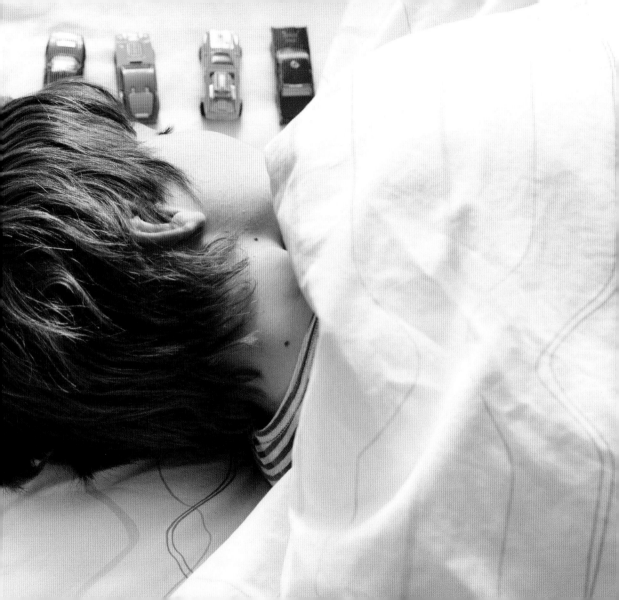

Giggle.

7 SILLY THINGS TO DO WITH YOUR KIDS

1. Send something unusual through the mail: Affix an address and postage to a Frisbee, a ball, a flip-flop—or anything else you can think of!

2. Make shadow puppets.

3. Mix two boxes of cornstarch with a container of shaving cream for messy, silly (outdoor) fun.

4. Thumb wrestle.

5. Make goofy faces with a flashlight under your chin.

6. Shuffle across the rug in stocking feet on a dry winter day and then try to touch each other—shocking!

7. Videotape yourselves making dinner as if you were on a cooking show.

enjoy the ride

Fun matters.

Fun relaxes and refreshes us, and connects us to others in a joyful way. Playtime exists outside of schedules and routines, engaging us creatively and sharpening our problem-solving skills. Rather than robbing us of energy, a rousing recess break increases it!

Show off
your wild side.

if it's in your way, climb over it

Children are the proverbial drops of water that eventually wear away boulders. "No" is never the end of a conversation, it's just a temporary hurdle. The initial "Why?" never elicits enough information; it's always followed by another. Understanding that perseverance is often the difference between winning and losing, kids press on with limitless spunk and resolve.

Kids don't equate failing with failure and they take stumbles in stride. Optimistic and resilient, they never see boundaries—just obstacles to be overcome.

The harder the wind blows, the higher your kite will fly.

Don't sit
down until
the game
is over.

You have
to eat a lot
of cereal
before you
find the
free toy.
Kellogg's
CORN FLAKES

Even babies grab for things just beyond their reach.

"Our fearlessness shall be our secret weapon."

—JOHN GREEN,
THE FAULT IN OUR STARS

Remarkably, Karina sustained only a few scratches and insect bites.

Unbeknownst to her father, three-year-old Karina Chikitova trailed after him when he left their home in the remote Sakha Republic to hike to his native village. But it wasn't long before Karina found herself lost and alone in the Siberian wilderness. For eleven days and nights, she hid from wolves and bears in tall grass, eating berries and drinking river water until she was finally found unharmed. The doctor who treated Karina said that her independence, strong will, and Siberian upbringing meant that she was not afraid to be alone in the woods, and knew how to survive.

Hang on TIGHT.

Practice until you can whistle.

10 TRICKY THINGS TO TRY TO MASTER WITH YOUR KIDS

1. Hula-hooping
2. Using chopsticks
3. Doing a cartwheel
4. Catching a snowflake on your tongue
5. Skipping stones
6. Shuffling and dealing cards like a pro
7. Hanging a spoon off your nose
8. Doing a yo-yo trick
9. Making a paper airplane
10. Whistling with a blade of grass

If you want a kitten,
start out asking for a horse.

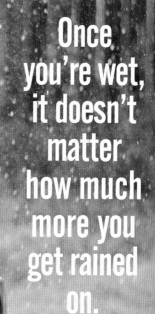

Once you're wet, it doesn't matter how much more you get rained on.

If you can't find a way through the crowd, make one.

Sometimes you have to take the test before you've finished studying.

Crawling still gets you there.

Just keep going.

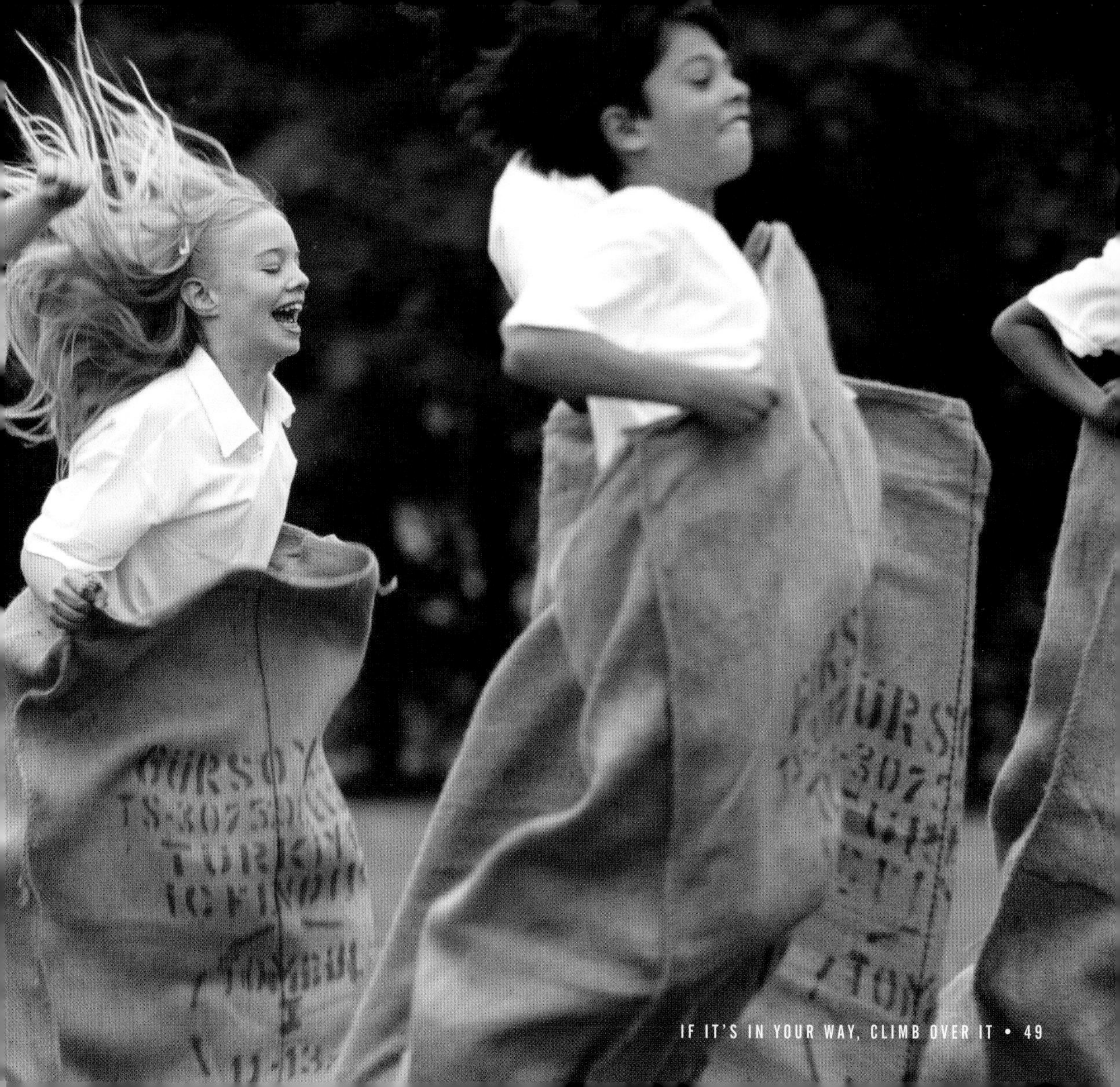

Even Superman probably tries to fly higher and faster.

"'You've got to be able to make those daring leaps or you're nowhere."

—RUSSELL HOBAN,
THE MOUSE AND HIS CHILD

Just keep BANGING until someone opens the door.

Don't argue for a later bedtime while you're wearing pajamas with feet.

Ask why until you understand.

Parents won't be surprised to learn that young children ask an average of 300 questions a day. Four-year-old girls top the list at 390, which averages out to about one question every two minutes. (Nine-year-old boys ask the fewest questions—although theirs frequently stump their parents!)

A Japanese business technique called the Five Whys mimics a child's persistence in getting to the crux of an issue. Developed in the 1930s by Sakichi Toyoda, the problem-solving tool involves asking "Why" five times in the belief that digging deeper and challenging conventional wisdom will reveal the true reason things are done a certain way, thus helping to determine if change is needed.

look at things
upside down

To a child, anything is possible—magic and miracles, dreams coming true, and fairy-tale endings. An afternoon spent looking up at the clouds is not wasted time—it's a free-spirited romp through the imagination, a reflection on all of the things that could be.

Children see things we can't because they look for things we don't. They soak up new information and adapt quickly and cleverly to changing circumstances. When it unexpectedly starts to rain, a child doesn't dash inside; she looks up at the sky, spreads her arms, and embraces her new, delightful reality.

Go in with your eyes open.

Make your own magic.

It's more fun
to color outside
the LINES.

LOOK AT THINGS UPSIDE DOWN • 63

Sometimes you find the neatest dragonfly when you're out looking for tadpoles.

Make up the rules as you go along.

When you're dressed up like a princess, it's easier to act like one.

Little ones spend up to two thirds of each day in imaginative play. But it's not all fun and games; as they play, they're honing their problem-solving skills. Studies have shown that pretend play encourages children to entertain a wide variety of possible solutions to real-life challenges and then predict the likely outcomes of each. This kind of uninhibited thinking can lead to unique and innovative solutions to problems that come up in everyday life.

Look behind the puppet theater

How do you know you can't make an airplane out of tinfoil and cardboard boxes unless you try?

You can teach an old dog new tricks with the right kind of treats.

Be curious.

"The whole world is full of things, and somebody has to look for them."

—ASTRID LINDGREN,
PIPPI LONGSTOCKING

Emelia hopes to become a paleontologist someday.

When she was just five years old, fossil hunter Emelia Fawbert embarked on her first excavation and unearthed the vertebra of a giant rhinoceros that roamed parts of England 50,000 years ago. Emelia found the vertebra poking up through the gravel and—with a little help from her dad—used a trowel to pry it out. Although several other fossils were discovered during the hunt, Emelia's was the most impressive!

Toads aren't ugly—they're just toads.

There are a lot of different ways to get to the top of the jungle gym.

Why do children see a world of possibilities that adults don't? Because in order to move efficiently through each day, we take mental shortcuts, using everything we already know to solve problems quickly. We don't stop to entertain a wide variety of original ideas because it's not practical.

To view the world from a child's fresh perspective, we need to give ourselves permission to get distracted and to daydream. And we should let ourselves consider ideas that are odd—or even downright kooky—without worrying about how other people will react. Just like kids do.

It can't hurt
to ask for a
fourth wish.

CHECK **UNDER** THE BED.

Lose yourself in another world.

make waves

A child is always searching for his inner superhero. He wants to put on the cape and do the right and brave thing. Believing that life should be fair and that good deeds should be rewarded and bad ones punished, a child will take a stand, hands on hips, and hold firm.

A child's moral code is unambiguous: There are no murky excuses or shifting rules. It *does* matter who started it. If the path in front of him doesn't go where he thinks it should, he'll strike off in a different direction and make his own way. He's not afraid to be first, and he won't look back to see if anyone has followed him.

Be the first one to make footprints in new snow.

It's not really giving if you only give away the animal crackers with missing heads and feet.

JUST DO YOUR BEST.

It doesn't really count if you're swinging the highest because you're getting pushed.

You'll never catch
a frog if you're worried about
getting your shorts wet.

Try the grown-up rake before you decide to use the kid rake.

Katie shows off one of her cabbages.

When she was in third grade, Katie Stagliano brought a cabbage seedling home from school and planted it in her backyard. She tended it daily and watched it grow into a forty-pound cabbage. When she brought it to a local soup kitchen, it fed 275 people! Inspired, she planted a vegetable garden at her school to help feed people in her community. Seven years later, she has eighty gardens in twenty-nine states, and her organization, Katie's Krops, has donated thousands of pounds of fresh vegetables to those in need.

Picking your nose when no one is looking is still picking your nose.

Nobody
can pedal
the bike
for you.

It's easier to see the mistakes on someone else's paper.

You can't stop the sled halfway down the hill.

If you're going to take just one step, make it a **giant** step.

Together we are better.

When a child knows something, she tells all of her friends about it. And then they tell *their* friends. Kids don't hoard knowledge, hoping to gain a competitive advantage over others; they share it. Thank goodness, because sharing information and collaborating effectively has helped humans survive and evolve. So the next time a child asks you to "Guess what?" listen up. Then pass it on.

sign your name BIG

A child is her own champion. She'll tell you how fast she can run, how well she can draw, and how quickly she can add numbers in her head. She won't apologize for her shortcomings or point out her deficiencies: Her focus is on all of the things she does well.

In a competitive world, the idea of front-loading pluck and confidence isn't a bad one. After all, many limitations are self-imposed. Because they don't hear a negative inner voice predicting failure, kids are willing to try just about anything. And sometimes, just believing you can makes all the difference.

Find a way

to stand out.

Speak up!

Little kids have a refreshing lack of awareness and concern about what others think of them. Because they're not afraid of being embarrassed or ridiculed, they are free to ask offbeat questions and entertain all sorts of unconventional ideas. Like jazz musicians improvising, they are spontaneously creative and free of inhibitions. By considering an issue from every possible angle—with no regard to practicality—kids often come up with remarkably clever ideas. And that's why every brainstorming session should include a few participants under the age of five.

If the flowers you draw don't look like anyone else's, that's GOOD.

ASK FOR
sprinkles.

Jump right in or you might change your mind about swimming.

Little crayons still make bright marks.

Alex with a pitcher of lemonade

Just before Alexandra ("Alex") Scott's first birthday, she was diagnosed with neuro-blastoma, a rare form of childhood cancer. When she was four, Alex decided to open a lemonade stand to raise money for cancer research. Her first effort brought in $2,000. For the next four years, Alex regularly set up lemonade stands and encouraged others to do the same. In 2004, Alex lost her battle with cancer; she was just eight years old. But in the years since then, the organization bearing her name, Alex's Lemonade Stand Foundation, has provided over 475 medical research grants and raised more than $100 million in the pursuit of her dream to eradicate childhood cancer.

Sometimes your best move is blocked by your own checkers.

Build the base of your block tower wider than the top.

If you wait until you're really sure, you'll never take off the training wheels.

Let's face it: Kids are not prepared for most of what life dishes out. They lack the maturity, experience, and sometimes even the physical capability to tackle new challenges with confidence. And yet they routinely sign on for advanced activities before they've met the prerequisites. Most of the time that leap of faith pays off, and they figure things out as they go along. They seem to understand that often, if you wait until you are thoroughly prepared, you miss your chance.

Don't
wait to be
discovered.

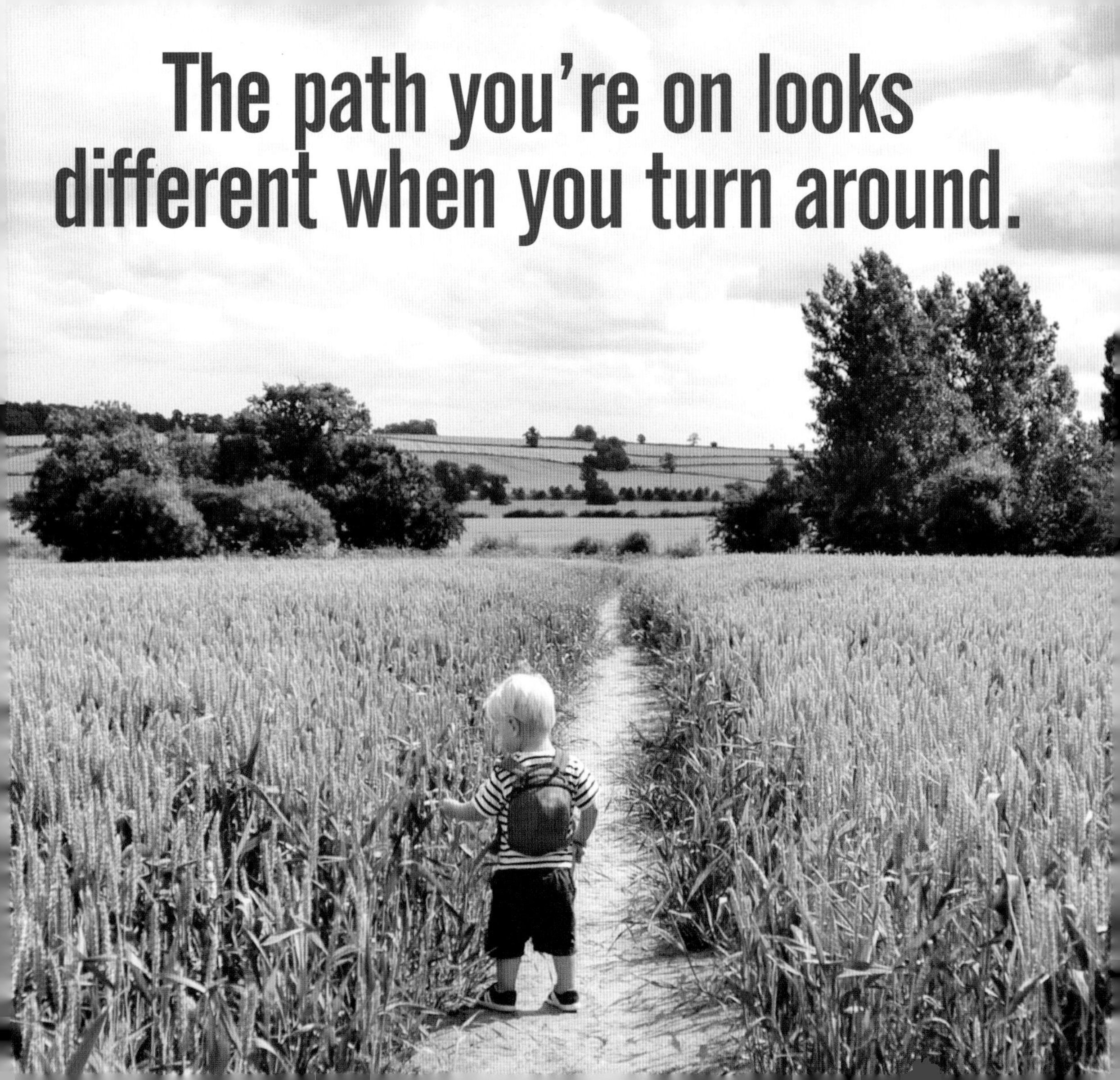
The path you're on looks different when you turn around.

You don't have to be able to spell to write a good story.

As Alec Greven watched other third-grade boys trying to get the attention of girls on the playground at his Colorado elementary school, he noticed what worked and what clearly didn't—and then decided to jot down some advice for his friends. According to Alec, girls don't like show-offs, the class clown, or boys who are sloppy. Another of his suggestions? "Don't act desperate." His observations became a pamphlet that was sold at his school's book fair, which caught the attention of a local television affiliate.

Alec advises his readers: "Control your hyperness."

After appearing on *The Ellen DeGeneres Show*, he was offered a book contract by HarperCollins. *How to Talk to Girls* went on to become a *New York Times* bestseller!

You feel a lot braver the *second* time you jump out of the tree.

Just because you're wearing COWBOY BOOTS doesn't mean you can ride a horse.

If you stand on tiptoe to be measured this year, you'll have to stand on tiptoe for the rest of your life.

invite
yourself
over

a little kiss can make a BIG difference

Little children love us just as we are, not as we should be. Quick to forgive and move on, they don't tally mistakes or hold grudges. They love us when we're at our worst (which is when it means the most). Naturally empathetic, kids respond quickly to anyone in need—and they understand that even a small gesture can have a big impact.

Kids instinctively know how to build and maintain relationships. Childhood friendships can sprout suddenly from a shared interest in tractors or cartwheels or the color purple. And though kids may initially bond over a trivial connection, friendships formed in elementary school can—and often do—last a lifetime.

Wave to people you don't know.

Every time
you pass him,
pat the dog.

trust people

Don't pop someone else's bubble.

If you kick the ball to another kid, he'll probably kick it back.

Little tykes have a knack for making new friends. They effortlessly start conversations with strangers, slip confidently into a game in progress, and even find ways to communicate with children who don't speak the same language. But what looks like a simple process is actually quite sophisticated. A child is able to quickly assess whether a potential playmate is trustworthy and supportive, and how this new friend seeks to influence him: Is she aggressive, or gently persuasive? By subconsciously running through this mental checklist, a child is able to connect with someone who will keep his secrets and laugh at his jokes, but who won't bully him into going down the slide headfirst or eating an earthworm.

If you're going to fight, use pillows.

Crying gets
you more
attention . . .

. . . but not
more friends.

"Love isn't how you feel. It's what you do."

—MADELEINE L'ENGLE,
A WIND IN THE DOOR

5-MINUTE IDEAS FOR SPREADING KINDNESS WITH YOUR KIDS

1. Tape quarters to a vending or gumball machine for the next person to use.

2. Leave a snack in the mailbox for the mail carrier.

3. Write positive messages on Post-It notes and leave them for strangers to find.

4. Leave a good book you've already read on a bus or park bench for someone else to find (with a note inside saying, "Enjoy this book!").

5. Write a letter to someone who needs encouragement.

When you bring a salamander to school, you find you have LOTS of friends you didn't even know about.

Rest your head on the nearest lap.

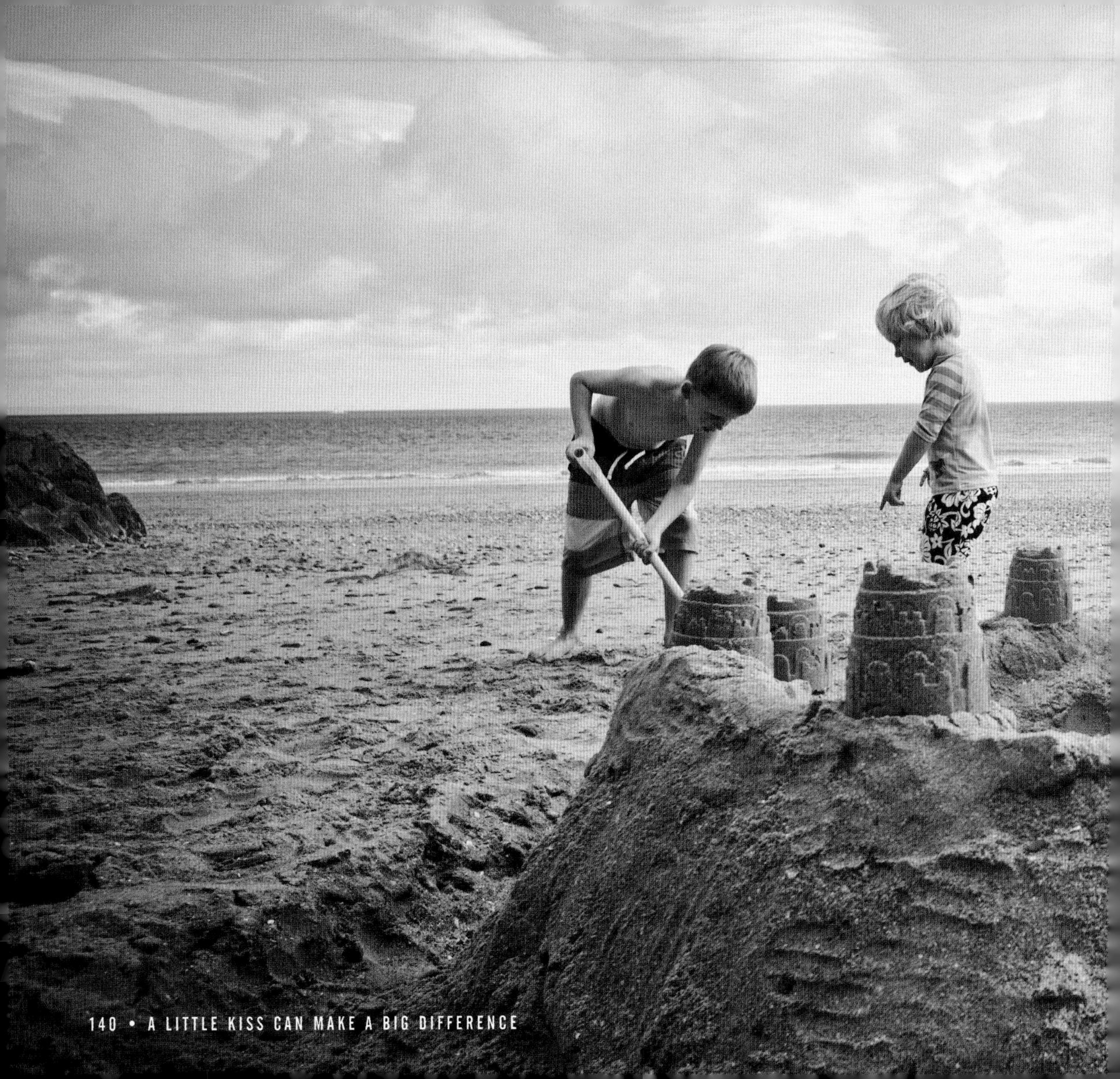

If you want to make a friend at the beach, start building a really big sand castle.

Stick
up for
your
brother.

Don't squeeze your hamster.

"'Sometimes,' said Pooh, 'the smallest things take up the most room in your heart.'"

—A.A. MILNE,
WINNIE-THE-POOH

7

pants with pockets are better

Bluntness is one of the things kids do best. They don't think about how their words will land, they simply observe life and say what they see, with no hidden agendas or ulterior motives. And though their honesty can lead to some awkward moments, it's also very refreshing.

Their observations help them understand how things work, as they struggle to connect pieces of information and formulate theories. They've learned that people are more likely to notice when they do something wrong than when they do something right. They've figured out that it's okay to cry, but it rarely solves the problem at hand. They've realized that in order to be brave, something a little scary has to happen first. And they know that no matter where they are—even Disneyland—they will always be glad to get home.

You can try on your father's shoes, but you can't walk very well in them.

Even if you make a really nice place for it to live with grass, dirt, and a few sticks, the caterpillar will still spend all of its time trying to get out of the jar.

the fuzzier, the better

You have to be ready to jump when the rope swings under your feet.

When Aniyah Rigmaiden started choking on a piece of apple during lunch, six-year-old Elspeth "Beanie" Mar leaped up and performed the Heimlich maneuver, which dislodged the apple. Beanie then asked her best friend, "Did I save your life?" Aniyah replied, "Yeah, you did!" Satisfied, Beanie sat back down and finished her lunch. The principal later remarked, "To us, it's incredible; to her, it was just the right thing to do."

Beanie (left) learned the Heimlich maneuver from watching the Disney Channel.

Whether
you're
in or
out, you
usually
want to
be the
other.

Sometimes you need a Saturday on a Wednesday.

Three hops get you just as far as one leap.

Kids know that little changes can yield big results. In fact, sometimes a tiny tweak is more effective than a huge, disruptive shift. Studies have shown, for example, that simply increasing the amount of time kids spend at outdoor recess helps them retain information and improves their grades.

Revamping the public education system? Overwhelming. Ten more minutes on the playground? Easy.

Sometimes
two is a crowd.

Food tastes better at a picnic.

There's always a
fancier skateboard...

but who needs it?

You only go down the slide headfirst once.

Wearing a halo can give you a headache after a while.

There is no good reason why clothes have to match.

Children say what they see. They state the obvious. This may seem naive and pointless to adults, but quite often, statements about plain truths lead to real breakthroughs. While adults are furiously overthinking an issue, kids are underthinking it. After all, an idea doesn't need to be ingeniously complex or clever to be first-rate. In fact, the best ideas are usually ones that make us wonder, "Now why didn't I think of that?"

To make a
seesaw work . . .

. . . you have
to take turns
being down.

You're only little until someone **LITTLER** comes along.

It's hard to save the best for last.

ACKNOWLEDGMENTS: Thank you to my favorite editor and collaborator, Margot Herrera. Wise and warm, Margot understood how much this project meant to me and worked hard to preserve the spirit and sentiments of the original book. Margot and I have worked together for more than a dozen years, and I continue to be in awe of her remarkable insights and intellect.

Many thanks to the entire Workman team: Anne Kerman and Michael Dimascio for fantastic photo research, Jenny Davis and Lisa Hollander for their great design work, Kate Karol and Evan Griffith for their editorial acuity, and Patrick Scafidi and Lauren Southard for getting the word out.

And most of all, thank you to my children, who inspired me to write this book over twenty years ago. Having kids was the best decision I ever made, and watching them grow into extraordinary adults has been the joy of my life.

PHOTO CREDITS: age fotostock: Doable/a collectionRF p. 157; Stuart Fox pp. 2–3; Old Visuals p. 107; Grant Rooney pp. 24–25. **Associated Press:** Gene J. Puskar, p. 15; **Getty Images:** lina aidukaite/Moment p. 37; Sally Anscombe/Moment pp. 140–141; arabianEye p. 27; Archive Photos p. 54; Asiaselects p. 74; Martin Barraud/Stone p. 26; Bipolar/The Image Bank pp. 90–91; Blend Images - KidStock/Brand X Pictures pp. 50, 169; Joey Boylan/Vetta p. 134; Skip Brown/National Geographic p. 30; Buena Vista Images/The Image Bank pp. 104–105; Lotus Carroll/Moment p. 43; Laurie Castelli/Cultura p. 154; Angelo Cavalli/The Image Bank pp. 52–53; Victoria Caverhill/Adore Photography/Moment pp. 40–41; Gary S Chapman/Photographer's Choice p. 121; Nick Clements/The Image Bank pp. 48–49; Jasper Cole/Blend Images p. 137; Constance Bannister Corp/Archive Photos p. 70; Cooriander/Moment Select p. 61; Cultura/©JFCreatives/Riser pp. 62–63; Daly and Newton/The Image Bank p. 125; Bruno De Hogues/The Image Bank pp. 10–11; Ghislain & Marie David de Lossy/The Image Bank p. 97; Ghislain & Marie David de Lossy/Cultura p. 131; Catherine Delahaye/The Image Bank p. 129; Igor Demchenkov/iStockphoto p. 16; Claudia Dewald/E+ p. 128; Robert Doisneau/Gamma-Rapho/Getty Images pp. 100–101; Eric Dugan/Moment Open p. 130; Jon Feingersh/Blend Images pp. ii–iii, 28–29; Michael & Patricia Fogden/Minden Pictures p. 138; Fox Photos/Hulton Archive pp. 65, 68, 166; Ned Frisk/Blend Images p. 142; Phil Fisk/Cultura/Risa p. 89; Fuse p. 162; Andre Gallant/Photographer's Choice p. 17; Karl Gehring/The Denver Post p. 120; Julia Goss/Moment Open p. 9; Allan Grant/Time Life Pictures pp. 96, 122; Jodie Griggs/Moment Open p. 44; Jamie Grill/Tetra images p. 109; Jamie Grill/Iconica p. 150; Dennis Hallinan/Hulton Archive Creative pp. 46, 155; hannahargyle/RooM p. 119; Noel Hendrickson/Digital Vision pp. 110–111; Henglein and Steets/Cultura pp. 86–87; Zena Holloway/The Image Bank p. 60; Hulton Archive p. 151; ImagesBazaar p. 76; Keiji Iwai/Photographer's Choice pp. 72–73; JGI/Jamie Grill/Blend Images pp. i, 81; Jose Luis Pelaez Inc/Blend Images p. 88; Sean Justice/Photodisc p. 139; Keystone/Hulton Archive p. 113; Aaron Kiely/Moment Open p. 64; Christina Kilgour/Moment p. 58; Jamie Kingham/Cultura p. 159; Lambert/Archive Photos pp. 8, 114–115, 146; Harold M. Lambert/Lambert/Getty Images p. 12; Tanya Little/Moment p. 20; Nathan Marx/E+ p. 69; Mecky/The Image Bank pp. 160–161; Tom Merton/OJO Images p. 47; Dmitry Naumov/Moment p. 84; Jekaterina Nikitina/Moment Select p. 135; noelbesuzzi/RooM p. 99; Orlando/Hulton Archive p. 158; Owl Stories/Moment Open pp. 148–149; Paper Boat Creative/Stone p. vi; PeopleImages.com/Digital Vision p. 108; Jodi Pfunder/Moment pp. 6–7; Martin Puddy/Stone p. 33; Suzanne Puttman Photography/Moment p. 82; NI QIN/E+ p. 42; Tosca Radigonda/Stockbyte p. 55; REB Images/Blend Images p. 80; Andrew Rich/Vetta pp. 56–57; Kinzie Riehm/Image Source p. 167; Darren Robb/Photographer's Choice p. 126; sarawut/Moment p. 116; Saul/Hulton Archive p. 21; Chuck Schmidt/E+ p. 4; Muriel de Seze/Digital Vision pp. 22–23; Kelly Sillaste/Moment pp. 164–165; Ariel Skelley/Blend Images p. 98; SSPL/Hulton Archive Creative p. 36; Tom Stoddart/Hulton Archive p. 118; Carl Sutton/Hulton Archive p. 145; svetikd/E+ pp. 18–19; Tatyana Tomsickova Photography/Moment p. 92; David Trood/The Image Bank p. 39; Chris Ware/Hulton Archive p. 163; Werner Wolff/Time Life Pictures p. 79; Todd Wright/Blend Images p. 124; Carol Yepes/Moment Open p. 143; Natalie Young/Cultura/Riser p. 102. **David Lazar:** pp. 132–133. **National Geographic Creative:** Aung Pyae Soe pp. 34–35. **NewsCom:** Randall Benton/Sacramento Bee/ZUMAPRESS.com p. 153. **Stacy Stagliano:** p. 93. **Shutterstock:** Ilya Andriyanov pp. 94–95; Natalia Kirichenko p. 66. **SWNS:** p. 75. **YSIA/The Siberian Times:** p. 38.

COURTESY PHOTOS: Alex's Lemonade Stand: p. 112; Cindy Copeland: p. iv.